Introduction

We've created eight colorful plastic canvas boxes d_____ beads and stitched with yarn to store your favorite _____

You'll enjoy our unique boxes for storing playing cards and other game accessories. Store your pencils and pens in the art box, and keep your photos organized in the beaded photo box.

Our memory boxes will help you organize jewelry, souvenirs, sewing items and, of course, buttons, while adding a sparkle to your desk or dresser.

Number refers to page where design appears.

Front cover

Photo Box

Materials
1½ sheets 7-mesh plastic canvas
16 (6mm) amber glass beads
59 amber seed beads
38 brown seed beads
permanent adhesive, such as Gem Tac
4- x 6-inch piece of mat board or
40 holes x 26 holes unstitched piece of plastic canvas
photo to fit 2½" diamond-shape opening
worsted weight yarn:
light green   19 yds
white   14 yds
light yellow   13 yds
embroidery floss (6 strands):
white   3 yds
light yellow   2 yds

Instructions

1. Cut out lid, front and back, two sides and base (42 holes x 28 holes, unstitched).

2. Stitch, following charts.

3. Referring to Joining Boxes & Lids on page 16, join sides of box to base and to each other with white. Overcast front and side edges of box with white.

4. Overcast front and side edges of lid with white. Join lid to back of box with white.

5. Referring to lid chart for placement, attach seed beads with white embroidery floss and 6mm beads with yellow embroidery floss.

6. Using white embroidery floss, string together two amber seed beads, then one amber glass bead then one brown seed bead. Bring floss around brown seed bead and string back through remaining beads, Fig 1. Make four strings of beads. Referring to lid chart for placement, and using white embroidery floss, attach stringed beads to front of lid.

7. Glue 4- x 6-inch piece of mat board or stitch a 4- x 6-inch piece of plastic canvas to inside of lid on both sides and slide in photo.

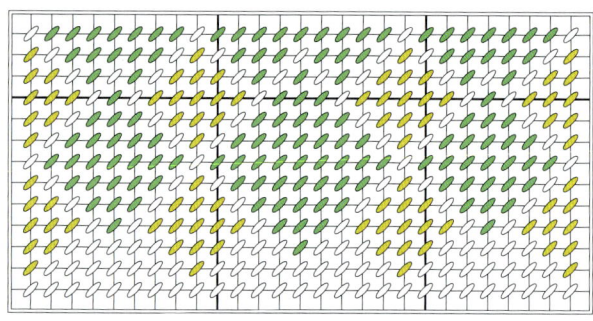

Sides
28 holes x 14 holes
Cut 2

COLOR KEY
Worsted Weight Yarn
- Light green
- Light yellow
- White
- Amber seed bead placement
- Brown seed bead placement
- Amber glass bead placement
- X Bead fringe placement

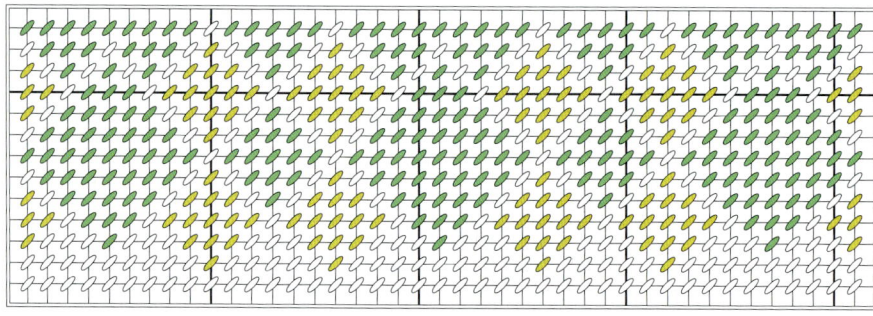

Front & Back
42 holes x 14 holes
Cut 2

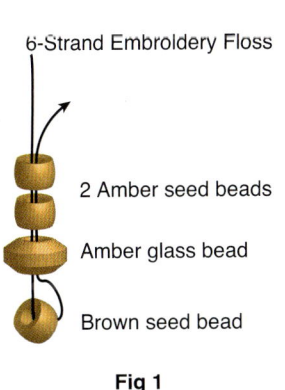

Fig 1
- 6-Strand Embroidery Floss
- 2 Amber seed beads
- Amber glass bead
- Brown seed bead

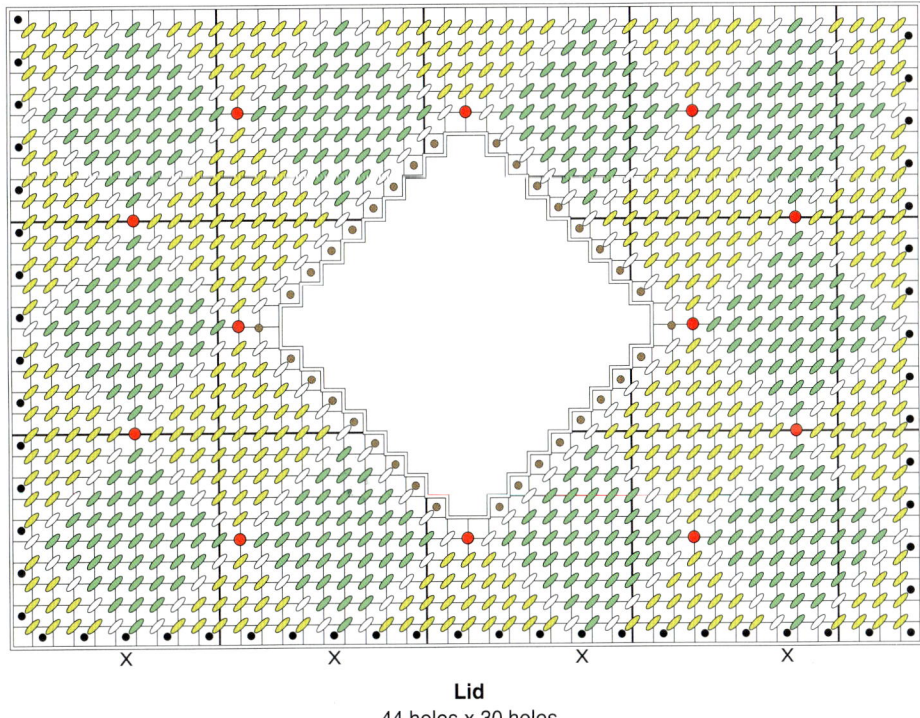

Lid
44 holes x 30 holes
Cut 1

Button Box

Materials
2 sheets 7-mesh plastic canvas
16 or more assorted buttons
worsted weight yarn:
yellow   38 yds
lime green   12 yds
rose   6 yds
embroidery floss:
blue   2 yds

Instructions

1. Cut out lid, four lid sides, four outer box sides, outer box base (29 holes x 29 holes, unstitched), inner box base (27 holes x 27 holes, unstitched) and four inner box sides (27 holes x 13 holes, unstitched).

2. Stitch, following charts. Work straight stitches last over previous stitching.

3. Referring to photo for placement and using embroidery floss, attach buttons to lid.

4. Referring to Joining Boxes & Lids on page 16, join lid sides to lid and to each other with yellow overcast stitches. Overcast remaining lid edges with yellow.

5. Join outer box sides to outer box base and to each other with yellow.

6. Join inner box sides to inner box base and to each other with yellow.

7. Overcast inner box with yellow.

8. Place inner box inside outer box and work overcast stitch through top edge of outer box and fourth row of inner box to join.

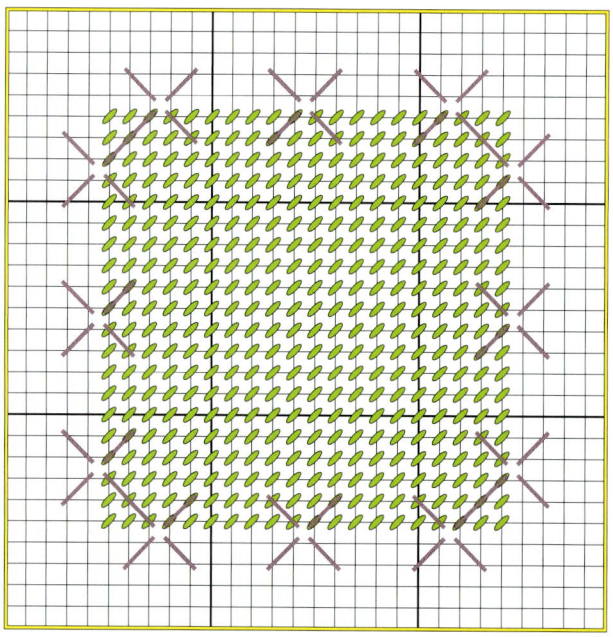

Lid
29 holes x 29 holes
Cut 1

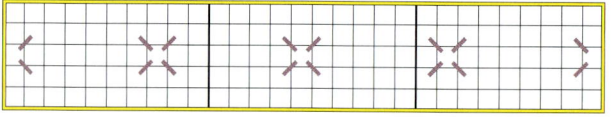

Lid Side
29 holes x 5 holes
Cut 4

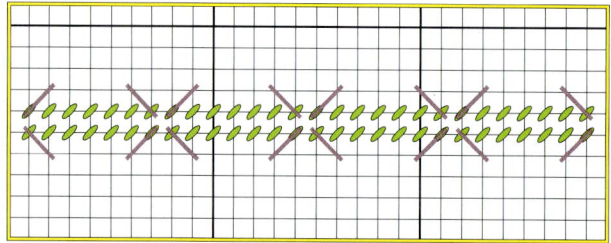

Outer Box Side
29 holes x 11 holes
Cut 4

COLOR KEY
Worsted Weight Yarn
- Lime green
  Uncoded areas fill with yellow Continental Stitch
- Rose Straight Stitch

Vintage Jewelry Box

Materials
2 sheets 7-mesh plastic canvas
16 (½-inch diameter) assorted white buttons
25 assorted white beads
permanent adhesive such as Gem Tac
worsted weight yarn:

black	27 yds
dk green	7 yds
off-white	7 yds
yellow	6 yds
lt green	6 yds
rose	5 yds
dk rose	5 yds

Instructions

1. Cut out lid, two lid long sides, two lid short sides, two outer box long sides, two outer box short sides, outer box base (32 holes x 29 holes, unstitched), inner box base (27 holes x 30 holes, unstitched), two inner box long sides (27 holes x 16 holes, unstitched) and two inner box short sides (30 holes x 16 holes, unstitched).

2. Stitch, following charts.

3. Snip off button shanks, and referring to photo for placement, glue buttons to lid with permanent adhesive.

4. Referring to photo for placement, glue beads to lid with permanent adhesive.

5. Referring to Joining Boxes & Lids on page 16, join lid sides to lid and to each other with black overcast stitches. Overcast remaining lid edges with black.

6. Join outer box sides to outer box base and to each other with black.

7. Join inner box sides to inner box base and to each other with black.

8. Overcast inner box with black.

9. Place inner box inside outer box and work overcast stitch through top edge of outer box and sixth row of inner box to join.

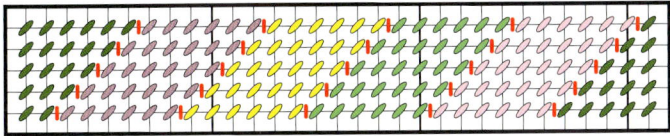

Lid Short Side
29 holes x 6 holes
Cut 2

Lid Long Side
32 holes x 6 holes
Cut 2

COLOR KEY
Worsted Weight Yarn
◢ Off-white
◢ Yellow
◢ Rose
◢ Dark rose
◢ Light green
◢ Dark green
◢ Black
◢ Black Backstitch

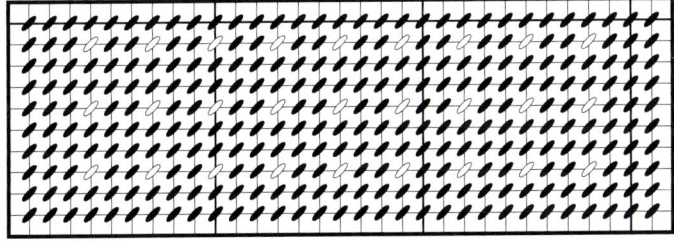

Outer Box Long Side
32 holes x 11 holes
Cut 2

American School of Needlework • Berne, IN 46711 • ASNpub.com • **Boxes with Buttons & Beads 5**

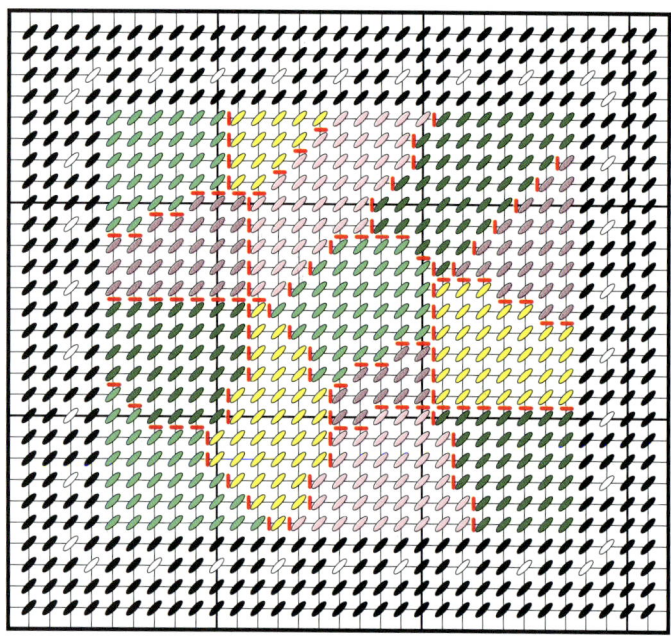

Lid
32 holes x 29 holes
Cut 1

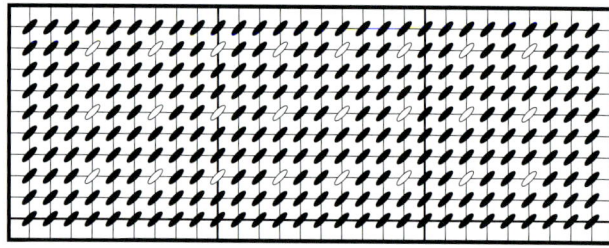

COLOR KEY
Worsted Weight Yarn
- Off-white
- Yellow
- Rose
- Dark rose
- Light green
- Dark green
- Black
- Black Backstitch

Outer Box Short Side
29 holes x 11 holes
Cut 2

Memory Box

Lid:
Materials
5" square wood keepsake box with 4½" square opening on top. **Note:** *Our photographed model was made with Crafty Productions Inc. Keepsake Décor Box #1KDW3.*
¼ sheet 7-mesh plastic canvas
31 (5mm) gold metallic pony beads
4 (¾-inch) brass corners (optional)
4 small finials for feet (optional) **Note:** *Our photographed model used ¼" finial dowel caps from Lara's Crafts #U11042.*
worsted weight yarn:

lime green	6 yds
lt green	6 yds
coral	5 yds
rose	4 yds
red	4 yds
yellow	3 yds

Instructions
1. Cut out lid.
2. Stitch, following chart.
3. Referring to chart for placement, attach beads using lime green yarn.
4. Overcast edges with lime green.
5. Stain wood box if desired.
6. Insert stitched piece into box inset.
7. Add brass corners and feet if desired.

Inner Box:
Materials
½ sheet 7-mesh plastic canvas
worsted weight yarn:

lt green	12 yds
dk green	9 yds
lime green	7 yds

Instructions
1. Cut out inner box base and four sides.
2. Stitch, following charts.
3. Referring to Joining Boxes & Lids on page 16, join inner box sides to inner box base and to each other with lt green, making sure right side of stitching is on inside of box. Overcast edges with lt green.
4. Insert inner box into wood box. Glue in place if desired.

COLOR KEY
Worsted Weight Yarn
- Yellow
- Coral
- Rose
- Red
- Light green
- Bead placement

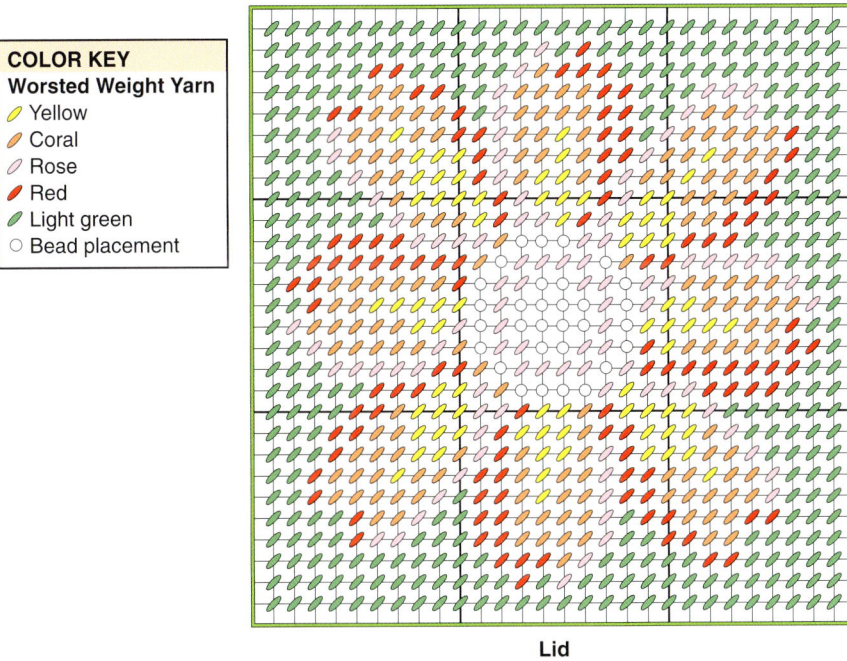

Lid
29 holes x 29 holes
Cut 1

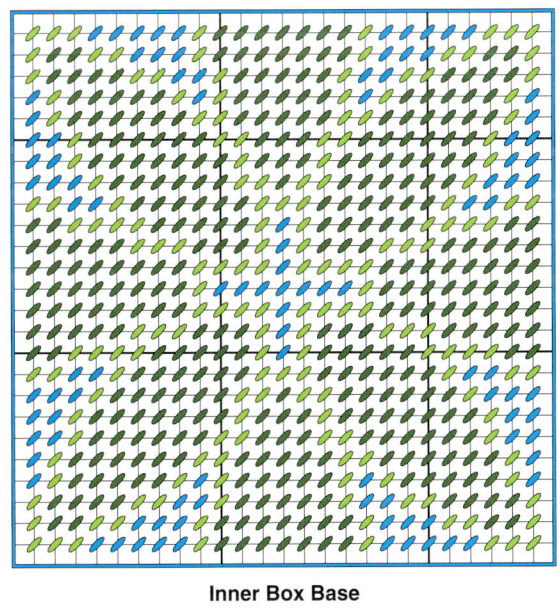

Inner Box Base
26 holes x 26 holes
Cut 1

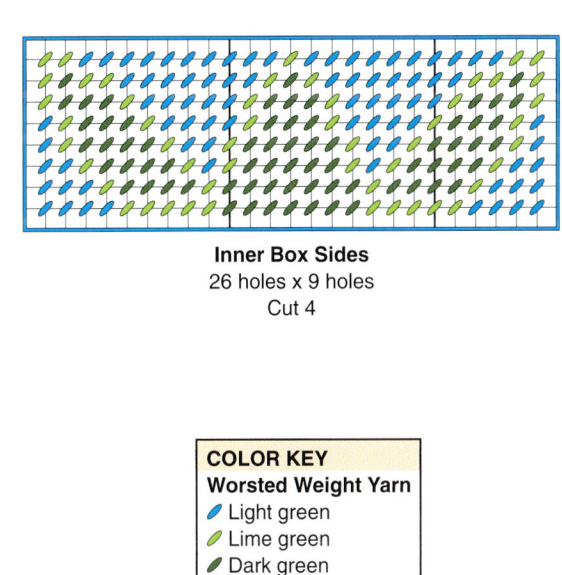

Inner Box Sides
26 holes x 9 holes
Cut 4

COLOR KEY
Worsted Weight Yarn
- Light green
- Lime green
- Dark green

Art Box

Materials
2 sheets 7-mesh plastic canvas
16 assorted buttons (optional)
worsted weight yarn:

white	22 yds
blue-green	17 yds
dk green	6 yds
pink	6 yds
orange	5 yds
black	5 yds
lt brown	4 yds
red	4 yds
yellow	4 yds
lime green	3 yds

embroidery floss:

blue	9 yds

Instructions

1. Cut out lid, two lid long sides, two lid short sides, two box long sides, two box short sides and box base (51 holes x 24 holes, unstitched).

2. Stitch, following charts. Work Backstitches and Straight Stitches last over previous stitching. For box long sides and box short sides, stitch bottom five rows with blue-green Continental Stitch.

3. Referring to photo for placement and using white yarn, attach buttons.

4. Referring to Joining Boxes & Lids on page 16, join lid sides to lid and to each other with white, making sure embroidered grid lines on lid short sides line up with embroidered grid lines on lid. One of the lid short sides will need to be turned upside down from the other to line up properly. Overcast edges with white.

5. Join box sides to box base and to each other with blue-green. Overcast edges with blue-green.

6. Place lid on box.

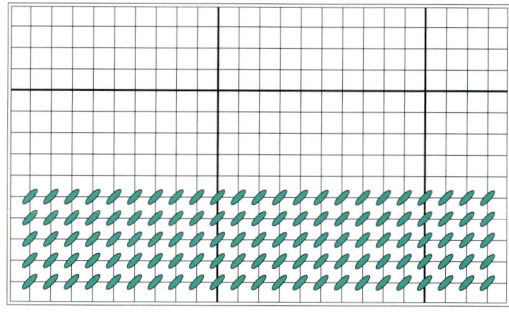

Short Side
24 holes x 14 holes
Cut 2

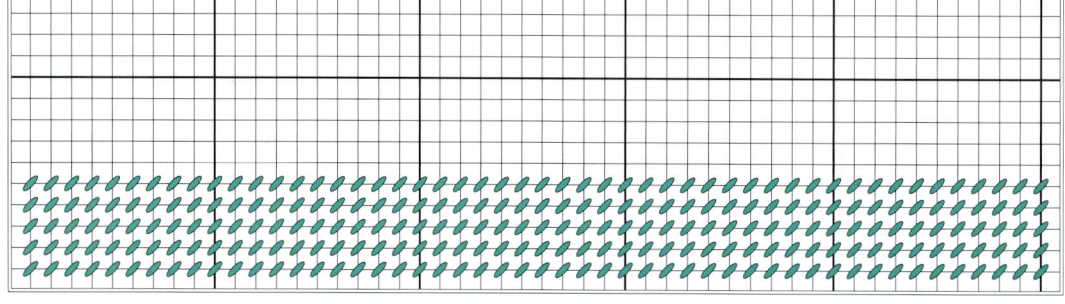

Long Side
51 holes x 14 holes
Cut 2

8 Boxes with Buttons & Beads • American School of Needlework • Berne, IN 46711 • ASNpub.com

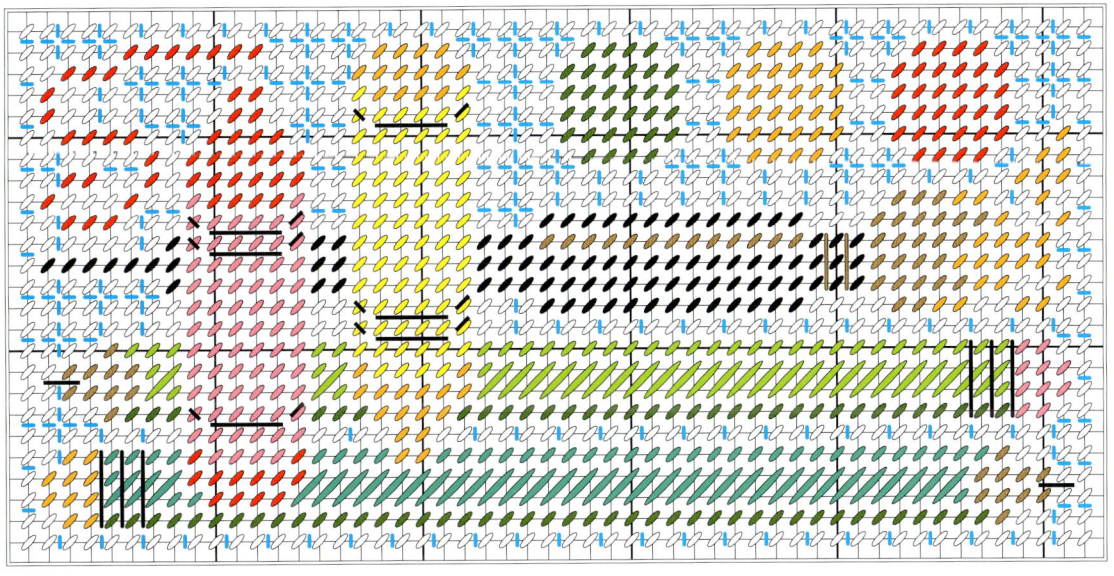

Lid
53 holes x 26 holes
Cut 1

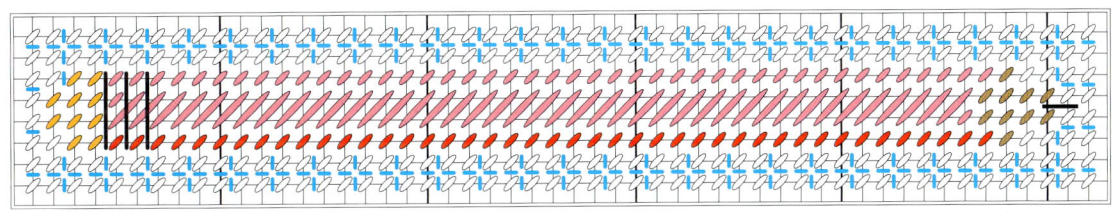

Lid Long Side
53 holes x 9 holes
Cut 2

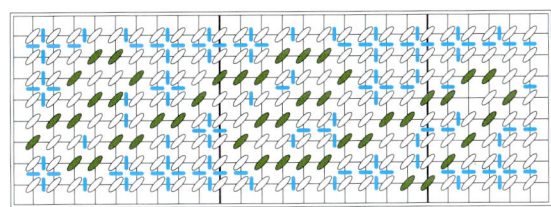

Lid Short Side
26 holes x 9 holes
Cut 2

COLOR KEY
Worsted Weight Yarn
- Yellow
- Orange
- Pink
- Red
- Lime green
- Blue-green
- Dark green
- Light Brown
- Black
- Light brown Straight Stitch
- Black Straight Stitch

Embroidery Floss
- Blue Backstitch

American School of Needlework • Berne, IN 46711 • ASNpub.com • **Boxes with Buttons & Beads 9**

Double-Deck Card Box

Materials
1½ sheets 7-mesh plastic canvas
32 (5-6mm) assorted colored plated beads
worsted weight yarn:
purple   21 yds
yellow   13 yds
coral   10 yds
red   10 yds
coordinating embroidery thread 2 yds

Instructions

1. Cut out lid, lid long side A, lid long side B, lid short side A, lid short side B, two base long sides (34 holes x 5 holes), two base short sides (26 holes x 5 holes) one center divider (24 holes x 4 holes) and base (34 holes x 26 holes, unstitched).

2. Stitch, following chart. Stitch base short sides, base long sides and center divider with purple Continental Stitch.

3. Referring to chart for placement, sew beads to lid with embroidery floss.

4. Referring to Joining Boxes & Lids on page 16, join lid sides to lid with yellow, using Braided Overcast Stitch, being careful to match color pattern.

5. Join lid sides to each other with yellow.

6. Overcast center divider with purple.

7. Join center divider to center bar of base with purple (Fig 1).

8. Join base sides to base using purple Braided Overcast Stitch (Fig 1).

9. Join base sides to each other with purple.

10. Overcast top edges of base using purple Braided Overcast Stitch.

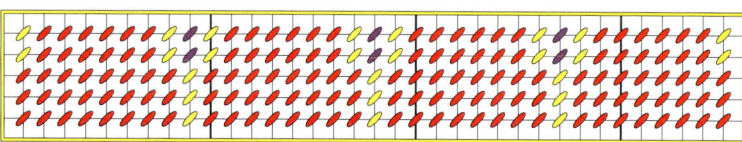

Lid Long Side A
36 holes x 6 holes
Cut 1

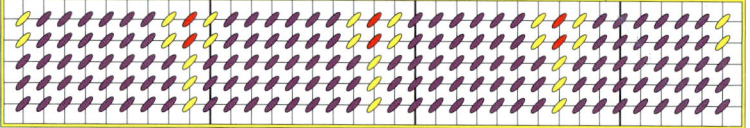

Lid Long Side B
36 holes x 6 holes
Cut 1

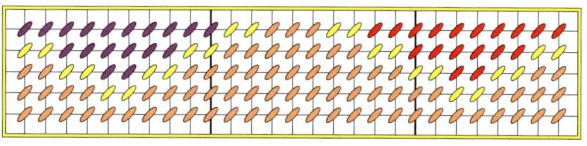

Lid Short Side A
28 holes x 6 holes
Cut 1

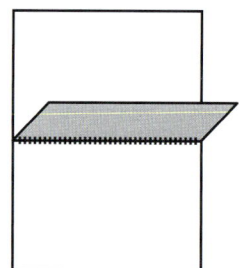

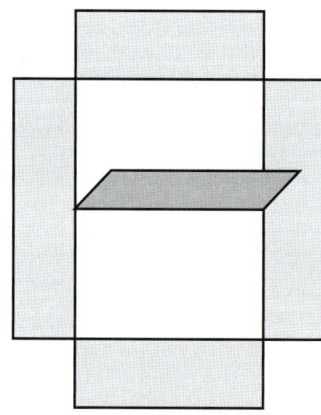

Fig 1

10 Boxes with Buttons & Beads • American School of Needlework • Berne, IN 46711 • ASNpub.com

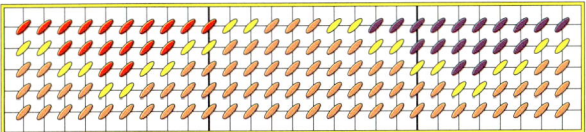

Lid Short Side B
28 holes x 6 holes
Cut 1

COLOR KEY
Worsted Weight Yarn
- Yellow
- Coral
- Red
- Purple
- Bead placement

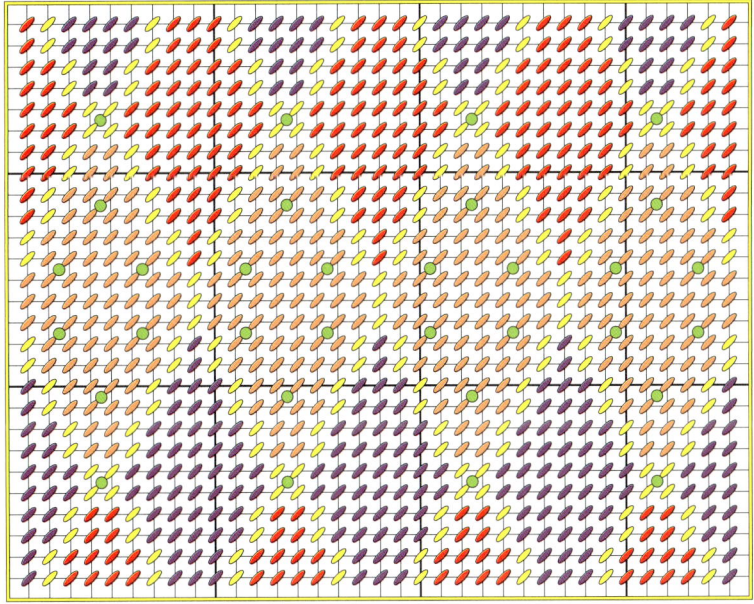

Lid
36 holes x 28 holes
Cut 1

Game Box

Materials
2 sheets 7-mesh plastic canvas
8 red and black buttons (optional) **Note:** Our photographed model used ½" red and black buttons and J. James Dress It Up card suit buttons.)
13 white seed beads
worsted weight yarn:
white	28 yds
lt blue	17 yds
red	10 yds
black	10 yds

embroidery floss:
black   2 yds

Instructions

1. Cut out lid, two lid long sides, two lid short sides, two box long sides, two box short sides and base (39 holes x 23 holes, unstitched).

2. Stitch, following charts. Work Backstitches last over previous stitching.

3. Referring to photo for placement, attach buttons to lid with matching color yarn. Using embroidery floss, attach seed beads to lid.

4. Referring to Joining Boxes & Lids on page 16, join lid sides to lid and to each other with white, making sure to match the checkerboard pattern. Overcast lid edges with white.

5. Join box sides to box base and to each other with white. Overcast box edges with white.

6. Place lid on box.

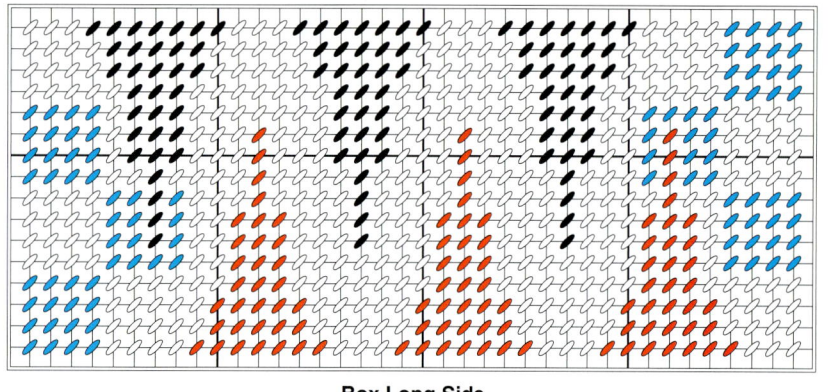

Box Long Side
39 holes x 17 holes
Cut 2

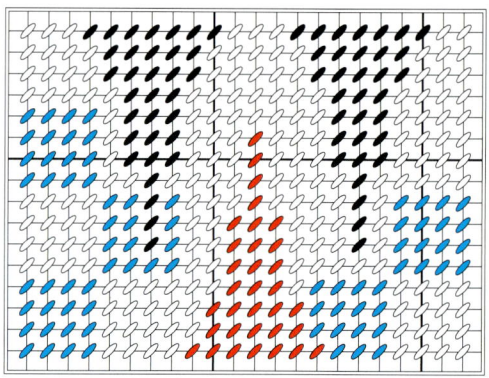

Box Short Side
23 holes x 17 holes
Cut 2

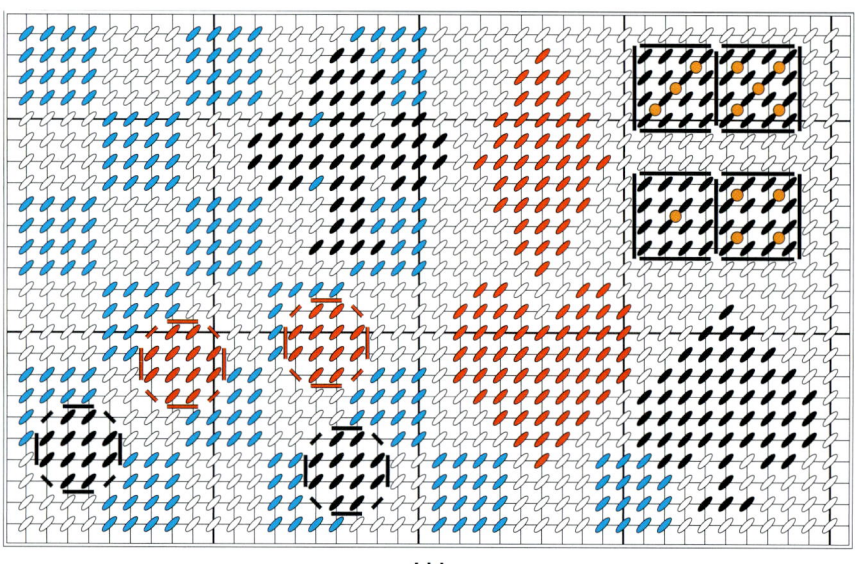

Lid
41 holes x 25 holes
Cut 1

COLOR KEY
Worsted Weight Yarn
- Blue
- Red
- Black
- Off-white
- Red Straight Stitch
- Black Straight Stitch
- White seed bead placement

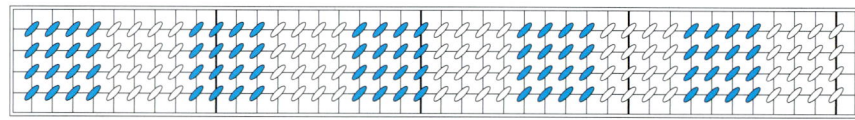

Lid Long Side
41 holes x 5 holes
Cut 2

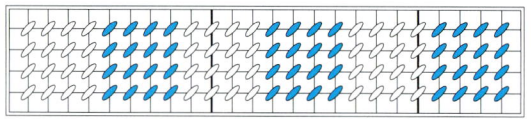

Lid Short Side
25 holes x 5 holes
Cut 2

Fun After 50 Box

Materials
1½ sheets 7-mesh plastic canvas
4½" straw hat
red spray paint
12 (½") red buttons
88 red E beads **Note:** Our photographed model used Westrim #4996 beads.
11 red bugle beads
permanent adhesive such as Aleene's Tacky Glue
bulky weight yarn:
purple   8 yds
Note: Our photographed model was made with Bernat Eye Lash, funky #35003.
worsted weight yarn:
purple   22 yds
embroidery floss:
purple   4 yds

Instructions

1. Cut out lid, box front, three box sides, latch and box base (31 holes x 31 holes, unstitched).

2. Stitch, following charts.

3. Referring to Joining Boxes & Lids on page 16, join box front and sides to box base and to each other with purple. Overcast front and side box edges with purple.

4. Sew six E beads through holes in 11 of the buttons and referring to chart for placement, glue buttons to box sides.

5. Referring to chart for placement, glue remaining button to latch. Alternate seven E beads with six bugle beads and attach to latch through lower holes of button. Alternate six E beads with five bugle beads and attach to latch through upper holes of button.

6. Overcast front and side edges of lid and join latch to front edge of lid with purple. Join back edge of lid to back of box.

7. Using embroidery floss, attach an E bead to edges of latch and lid in every other hole. Do not attach E beads where latch is joined to lid.

8. Paint straw hat red.

9. Glue two layers of eye lash yarn around crown of hat for hat band.

10. Center and glue hat to lid.

11. Gently scratch all fur yarn with fingernail to fluff up.

COLOR KEY
Worsted Weight Yarn
- Purple
- Purple Fur
- Unstitched

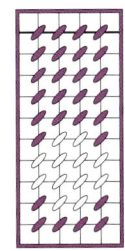

Latch
5 holes x 11 holes
Cut 1

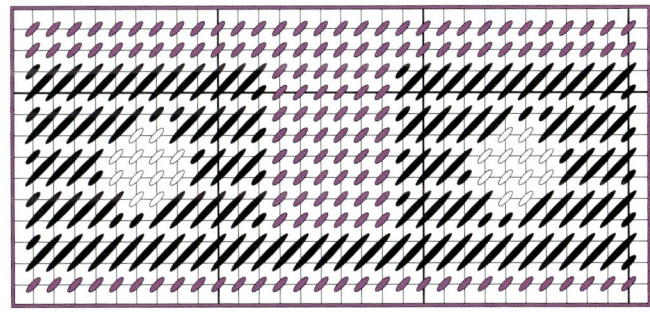

Box Front
31 holes x 14 holes
Cut 1

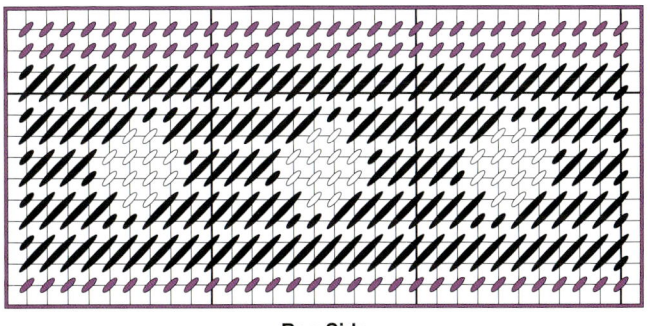

Box Side
31 holes x 14 holes
Cut 3

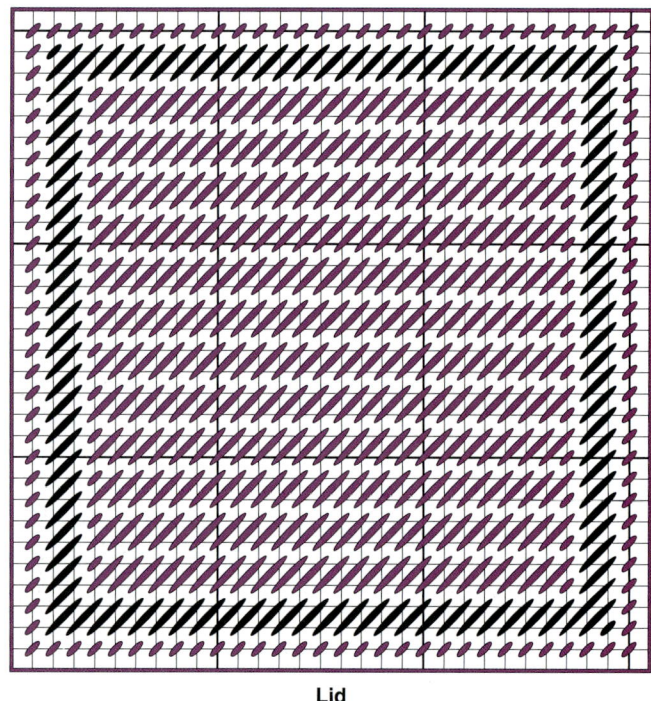

Lid
31 holes x 31 holes
Cut 1

COLOR KEY
Worsted Weight Yarn
▱ Purple
▱ Purple Fur
▱ Unstitched

General Directions

The Canvas Grid
All of these projects were worked on plastic canvas sheets, with seven stitches to the inch, called 7-mesh plastic canvas. We have used regular weight canvas, available in sheets measuring 10½ x 13½ inches.

Pattern Charts and Equipment
There is a pattern chart for most stitched pieces. The color keys indicate the color and type of stitch to use.

You will need a size 16 or 18 tapestry needle for stitching, a grease pencil or felt pen to mark the pattern shape on the plastic canvas, and strong scissors or a sharp craft knife to cut the canvas.

The Yarn
Any yarn that covers the canvas can be used with plastic canvas. We have used one strand of worsted weight yarn for the cover models. Use a 36-inch length of yarn for stitching; use an 18-inch length if the yarn tends to fray. There are approximately 70 yards per ounce of worsted weight yarn.

Cutting the Canvas
All of our patterns are measured by holes. Mark the outline of each piece on the plastic canvas and cut the pieces (Fig 1), using scissors or craft knife for small areas. Trim any plastic nubs and cut corners on the diagonal (Fig 2). Be careful not to cut so close that the corner is weakened.

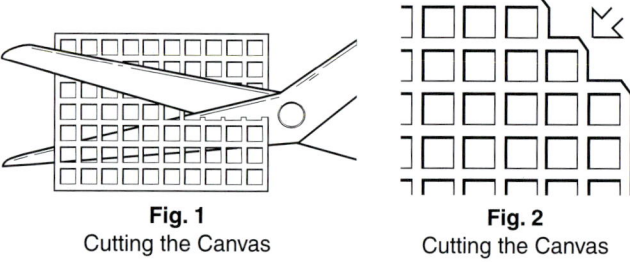

Fig. 1
Cutting the Canvas

Fig. 2
Cutting the Canvas

Beginning and Ending
Do not tie a knot to begin stitching with a new strand. Hold an inch of the end in place and work the first few stitches over the end (Fig 3). You may also anchor the end by running it through a few stitches of an adjacent stitched area. End strand by running it through the back of a stitched area and trim it closely on the wrong side of canvas.

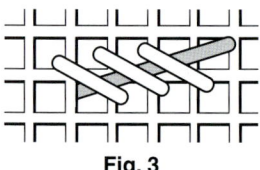

Fig. 3
Beginning & Ending Yarn

The Stitches

Continental Stitch
Most designs are worked in Continental Stitch. This forms a flat diagonal stitch on the front of the canvas. To work rows, bring the needle up through the canvas at odd numbers and down at even numbers (Fig 4). The rows can be worked from right to left or left to right; notice the difference in numbering, depending on the direction of the work.

Some designs may require a Reverse Continental Stitch where the stitches slope in the opposite direction. To work rows (Fig 5) bring needle up through canvas at odd numbers, down at even numbers.

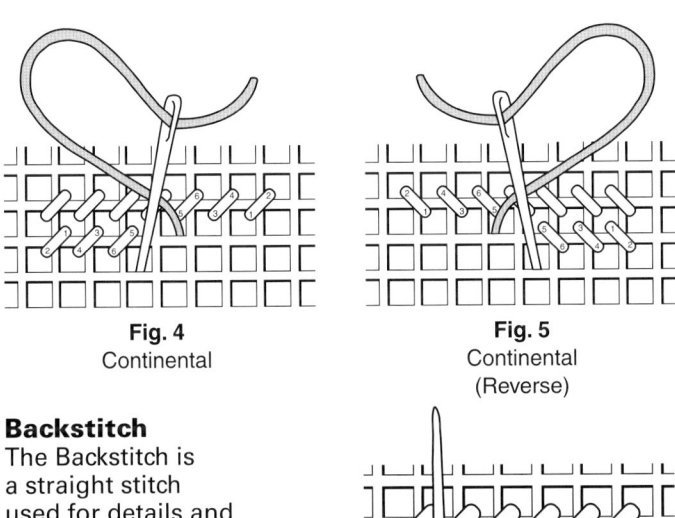

Fig. 4 Continental

Fig. 5 Continental (Reverse)

Backstitch
The Backstitch is a straight stitch used for details and decoration, worked on top of an area of completed stitching. It is worked over one bar in any direction (Fig 6). The placement of the stitches will be indicated on the chart.

Fig. 6 Backstitch (Over previous)

Straight Stitch
Straight stitches can be made in any direction and over one or more bars; direction will be noted on the chart. They can be used for details and decorations worked on top of an area of completed stitching. Bring needle up at one end of the stitch and down at the other end (Fig 7).

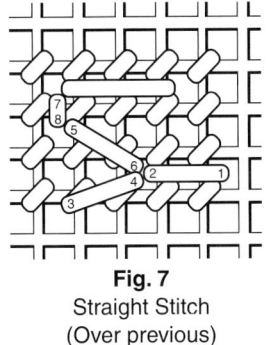

Fig. 7 Straight Stitch (Over previous)

Slanting Gobelin
The Slanting Gobelin (pronounced like "go"), is a long diagonal stitch that can be worked over any number of bars (Fig 8). Gobelin stitches are indicated by long lines showing the exact placement of each stitch with color references in the color key.

Reverse Slanting Gobelins slope in the opposite direction (Fig 9). The direction will be shown on the chart.

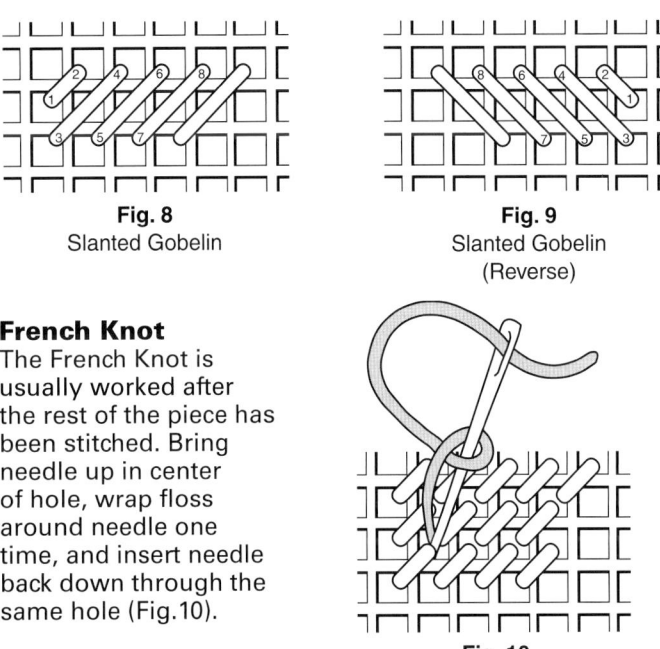

Fig. 8 Slanted Gobelin

Fig. 9 Slanted Gobelin (Reverse)

French Knot
The French Knot is usually worked after the rest of the piece has been stitched. Bring needle up in center of hole, wrap floss around needle one time, and insert needle back down through the same hole (Fig.10).

Fig. 10 French Knot

Overcast Stitch
This stitch is used in two ways; to finish canvas edges or to join two pieces of canvas. Work from left to right or right to left, whichever is more comfortable. To finish canvas edges, stitch loosely so strand will cover canvas (Fig 11). Take one stitch in each hole along a straight edge or into an inside corner, and three stitches when going around an outside corner. If the strand does not cover well, take additional stitches in each hole as needed.

To join two pieces, hold pieces together and line up matching holes. Start joining with a holding stitch through the first hole of the two pieces, then continue joining (Fig 12), going through both pieces with each stitch. When ending off strand, tie a knot or weave end in securely.

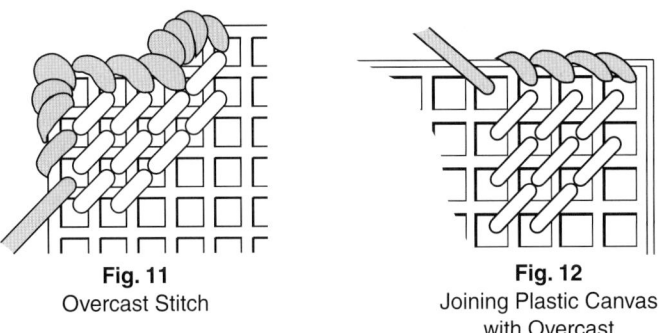

Fig. 11 Overcast Stitch

Fig. 12 Joining Plastic Canvas with Overcast

Braided Overcast Stitch

The Braided Overcast Stitch is a decorative stitch which can be used for overcasting or for joining two pieces (Fig 13). Bring needle down at 1, up at 2, down at 3, up at 4, down at 1, up at 2, down at 5, up at 6, down at 3, up at 4 and continue this pattern.

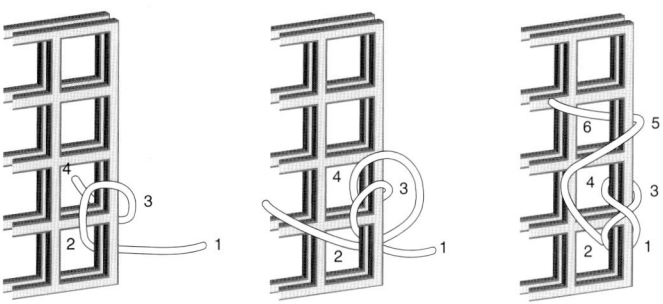

Fig. 13
Braided Overcast Stitch

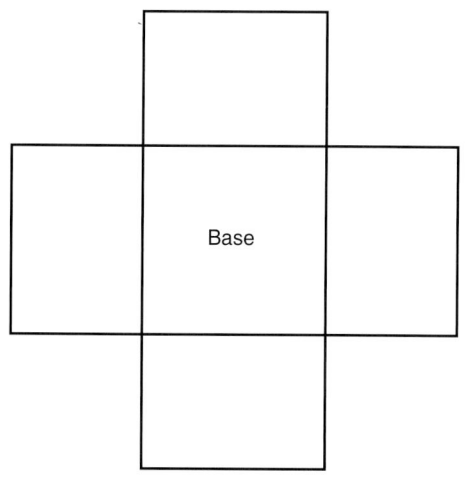

Fig. 14
Box Joining Diagram

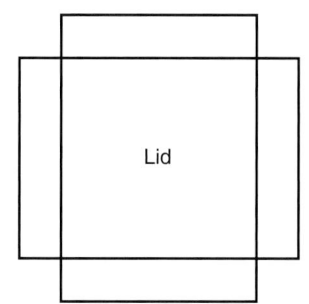

Fig. 15
Lid Joining Diagram

Joining Boxes & Lids

To join boxes, refer to photos and attach all four sides to base, making sure to follow the box pattern (Fig 14) and then join sides to each other.

Join lids in the same way (Fig 15) unless otherwise noted in the project instructions.

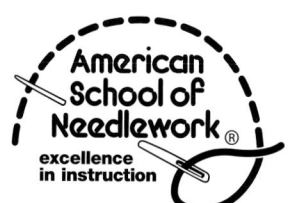

DRG Publishing
306 East Parr Road
Berne, IN 46711
©2005 American School of Needlework

TOLL-FREE ORDER LINE or to request a free catalog (800) 582-6643
Customer Service (800) 282-6643, Fax (800) 882-6643

Visit www.AnniesAttic.com

We have made every effort to ensure the accuracy and completeness of these instructions. We cannot, however, be responsible for human error, typographical mistakes or variations in individual work. Reprinting or duplicating the information, photographs or graphics in this publication by any means, including copy machine, computer scanning, digital photography, e-mail, personal Web site and fax, is illegal. Failure to abide by federal copyright laws may result in litigation and fines.

ISBN:1-59012-134-1   All rights reserved.   Printed in U.S.A.   1 2 3 4 5 6 7 8 9